Country File
Ireland

Michael March

FRANKLIN WATTS
LONDON•SYDNEY

First published in 2001 by
Franklin Watts
96 Leonard Street, London
EC2A 4XD

Franklin Watts Australia
56 O'Riordan Street, Alexandria
NSW 2015

COUNTRY FILE: IRELAND produced for Franklin Watts by
Bender Richardson White, PO Box 266, Uxbridge, UK.
Project Editor: Lionel Bender
Text Editor: Peter Harrison
Designer: Ben White
Picture Researcher: Cathy Stastny
Media Conversion and Make-up: Mike Pilley, Radius
Production: Kim Richardson

Graphics: Mike Pilley, Radius
Maps: Stefan Chabluk

For Franklin Watts:
Series Editor: Adrian Cole
Art Director: Jonathan Hair

A CIP catalogue record for this book is available
from the British Library.

ISBN 0-7496-4221-1

Dewey Classification 914.15

Printed in Dubai

Picture Credits

Pages: 1: James Davis Travel Photography. 3: PhotoDisc
Inc./Neil Beer. 4: Hutchison Photo Library/Crispin
Hughes. 6: James Davis Travel Photography. 7: PhotoDisc
Inc./Neil Beer. 8: Hutchison Photo Library/Tony Souter.
9: Hutchison Photo Library/P. Goycolea. 10 top:
PhotoDisc Inc./Neil Beer. 10–11 bottom: Hutchison
Photo Library/Crispin Hughes. 13: Hutchison Photo
Library/J. C. Tordai. 15: Eye Ubiquitous/Tim Page. 16:
Hutchison Photo Library/Tuck Goh. 18: Hutchison Photo
Library/Jeremy A. Horner. 20: Eye Ubiquitous/Paul
Seheult. 21: James Davis Travel Photography. 22–23: DAS
Photo/David Simson. 23 top: Eye Ubiquitous/Tim Page.
24: James Davis Travel Photography. 25: Hutchison Photo
Library/Tuck Goh. 26 top: James Davis Travel
Photography. 26 bottom: Hutchison Photo Library/Jeremy
Horner. 28: Hutchison Photo Library/Tuck Goh. 29: Eye
Ubiquitous/B. Gibbons. 30: PhotoDisc Inc./Neil Beer.
31: PhotoDisc Inc./Neil Beer.
Cover photo: PhotoDisc Inc./Neil Beer.

The Author
Michael March is a full-time writer and
editor of non-fiction books. He has
written more than 10 books for children
about different countries of the world.

Contents

Welcome to Ireland 4

The Land 6

The People 8

Urban and Rural Life 11

Farming and Fishing 12

Resources and Industry 14

Transport 16

Education 19

Sport and Leisure 20

Daily Life and Religion 22

Arts and Media 24

Government 26

Place in the World 28

Database 30

Glossary 31

Index 32

Welcome to Ireland

Ireland is an island in north-western Europe famous for the beauty of its landscape. It is 483 kilometres long and 274 kilometres across at its widest point, with some 5,000 kilometres of coastline. The rugged west coast overlooks the Atlantic Ocean. The east coast faces Great Britain across the North Channel, Irish Sea and St George's Channel.

The people of Ireland are mostly descended from the Celts and have their own Irish language and rich culture. Irish music and dance, which are sometimes loud, rousing and energetic, at other times quiet and thoughtful, are known and admired across the world. Ireland has also produced some of the world's great writers and poets, such as James Joyce and William Butler Yeats.

Two Irelands

Five-sixths of Ireland make up the Republic of Ireland, called in Irish, Éire. The remaining north-eastern corner is called Northern Ireland. Unlike the Republic, this is not an independent country but part of the United Kingdom (UK), which also includes Great Britain (England, Scotland and Wales). This book features the Republic of Ireland.

Ireland is often called the 'Emerald Isle' because the mild climate produces a rich, green landscape. Most of the land is used for farming. ▼

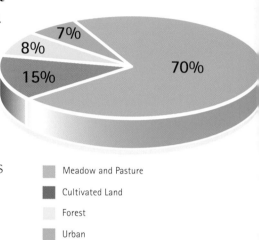

7%
8%
15%
70%

- Meadow and Pasture
- Cultivated Land
- Forest
- Urban

In Donegal, on the north-west coast, some families still live in traditional homes, with thatched roofs and stone fireplaces. ▼

ATLANTIC
OCEAN

N
W E
S

Aran Island

Donegal

BLUE STACK
MOUNTAINS
•Donegal

Donegal Bay

NORTHERN
IRELAND

55°N

Mayo

SLIEVE GAMPH

Sligo
○Sligo

Leitrim

Monaghan

Dundalk○

54°N

Dundalk Bay

Roscommon

Cavan

Longford

Louth

IRISH
SEA

Roscommon○

Meath

Galway

Athlone○

Westmeath

Galway○

Galway Bay

REPUBLIC OF

Kildare

Dublin□

ARAN
ISLANDS

IRELAND

Offaly

BOG OF
ALLEN

Kildare○

WICKLOW MOUNTAINS

Wicklow
MOUNTAINS

53°N

Lough Derg

Laois

Clare

Carlow○

Wicklow○

Shannon

SLIEVEFELIM
MOUNTAINS

Carlow

Maigue

Limerick○

Kilkenny

Barrow

Wexford

Limerick

Tipperary

Kilkenny○

Tipperary○

Suir

○Tralee

GALTY MOUNTAINS

Wexford○

Blackwater

Waterford

Waterford○

ngle Bay

Killarney○

Dungarvan○

52°N

Kerry

MACGILLYCUDDY'S
REEKS

Cork

Cork○

○Bantry

Bantry Bay

□ Capital   ○ Major cities and towns

Mountains   Grassland and farming

—— Country boundary   —— County boundary

0   50 Miles

0   75 Kilometres

5

10°W   9°W   8°W   7°W   6°W

The Land

The centre of Ireland is a large area of rolling bog. This region is rich in peat and pasture land. The landscape of Ireland's coastal areas includes valleys, mountains and rocky bays with long, sandy beaches.

The highest point in Ireland is the 1,041-metre-high summit of Carrantuohill in Macgillycuddy's Reeks, a mountain range in the south-west. Other mountain ranges include the Wicklow Mountains in the east, the Blue Stack Mountains in the north-west, and the Nephin Beg Range in the west.

Seen on a map, the west coast is irregular and dotted with islands. Along the coast, from County Donegal in the north to County Cork in the south, scenic bays such as Dingle Bay and Bantry Bay curve between spectacular cliffs that jut out into the Atlantic Ocean.

Wildlife

Animals include deer, squirrels, badgers, Irish stoat, Irish hare, mice, bats and a species of lizard, but snakes are unknown.

Shore birds, particularly waterfowl, and field birds are plentiful. Otters and mink inhabit the waterways.

Common and grey seals are found along the coasts, and dolphins live in inshore waters.

A sheltered harbour at Cobh in County Cork in the south of Ireland. ▼

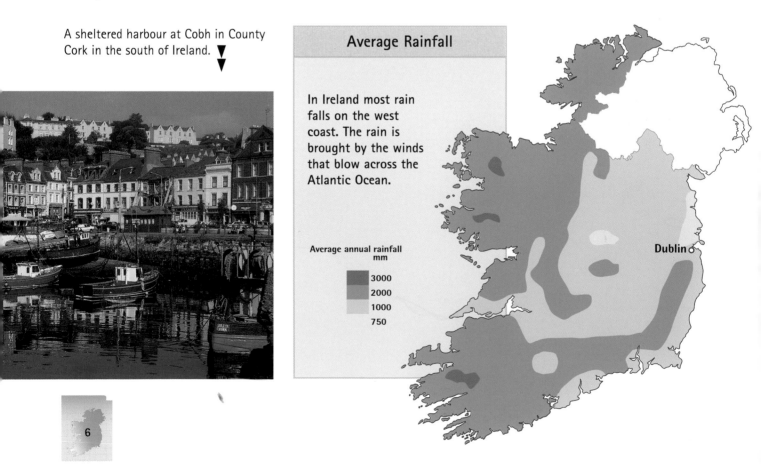

Average Rainfall

In Ireland most rain falls on the west coast. The rain is brought by the winds that blow across the Atlantic Ocean.

Average annual rainfall mm

- 3000
- 2000
- 1000
- 750

Dublin

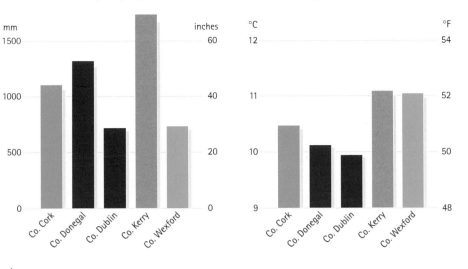

Rainfall (in a year)

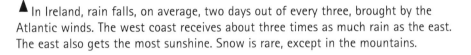

Temperature – Mean

Sunshine Hours – Daily Mean

In Ireland, rain falls, on average, two days out of every three, brought by the Atlantic winds. The west coast receives about three times as much rain as the east. The east also gets the most sunshine. Snow is rare, except in the mountains.

Rivers and climate

The mouth of the Shannon, Ireland's longest river, opens onto the Atlantic on the west coast, near the town of Limerick. The river starts its course in the northern lowlands, near Sligo Bay. Ireland's capital, Dublin, stands on the River Liffey, which rises in the Wicklow Mountains and meets the Irish Sea at Dublin Bay.

The warm waters of the North Atlantic Gulf Stream allow Ireland to enjoy mild winters while the country's northerly position makes for cool summers. Temperatures vary little across the country, ranging from about 3°C in winter to 18°C in summer.

Web Search ▶▶

▶ www.cso.ie/principal stats/pristat1.html
This Irish Government website page gives statistics for weather (as well as for population) in Ireland.

The remains of a prehistoric fort on Inishmaan, one of the Aran Islands near Galway Bay. ▼

The People

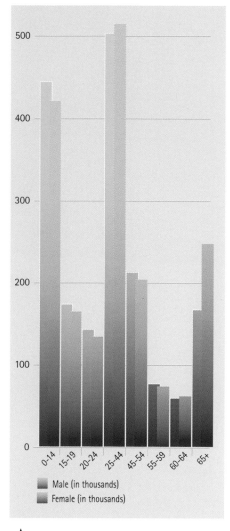

Ireland currently has around 3.7 million people. Most of these are descended from the Celts, who originally came from mainland Europe. A smaller number of Irish citizens have English or Norman (French) ancestors. In recent years, a few people from Asian and African countries have settled in Ireland.

The Irish people's Celtic ancestors invaded in the fourth century BC. They conquered the land and then blended with the local peoples, including the Firbolg and the Tuatha De Danann, whose names have passed into legend. The Celts were known as 'Milesians' because they were supposed to have been descended from the ancient King Milesius of Spain. They were also called Gaels, which is why the Irish language is known as Gaelic.

Male (in thousands)
Female (in thousands)

▲ The population of present-day Ireland is fairly young. Some 1.5 million Irish people are under the age of 25. About 70 per cent of Irish citizens are under 45.

A fisherman repairs his nets on a beach in County Cork. With such a long coastline and many rivers and lakes, the lives of many Irish people are linked to water. ►►

8

The Irish language

In Ireland today, Gaelic is used much less than English, though its use is increasing. Almost all Irish people speak English, compared to a little over a third of the population who speak both languages.

Most of those brought up to speak Irish come from the west of the country, to the north or west of the River Shannon. These regions are known as the Gaeltacht.

According to Ireland's constitution, Irish, not English, is the country's first official language, with English the second. All street names, signposts and public notices are displayed in both languages.

Since 1922, after Ireland gained its independence from the United Kingdom, Irish has been taught in all schools. Today, although Irish is still the minority language, it is more widely read, more widely spoken and more widely understood than at any time in the past century.

▲ Like these girls, many Irish people are fair-skinned. Females outnumber males by more than 25,000, but among those aged under 25 there are more males than females.

Web Search ►►

► www.cso.ie/principal stats/pristat2.html
This Irish government website gives precise population figures.

► www.ireland.org
Gives information about Irish history from the ancient past to recent times.

Population Density

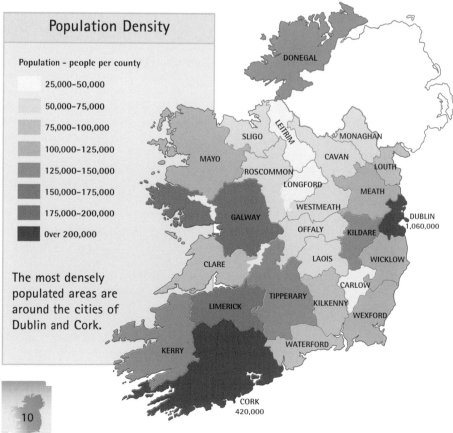

Population - people per county

25,000–50,000
50,000–75,000
75,000–100,000
100,000–125,000
125,000–150,000
150,000–175,000
175,000–200,000
Over 200,000

The most densely populated areas are around the cities of Dublin and Cork.

DONEGAL
SLIGO
LEITRIM
MONAGHAN
MAYO
CAVAN
ROSCOMMON
LOUTH
LONGFORD
MEATH
WESTMEATH
GALWAY
DUBLIN 1,060,000
OFFALY
KILDARE
LAOIS
WICKLOW
CLARE
CARLOW
TIPPERARY
KILKENNY
LIMERICK
WEXFORD
WATERFORD
KERRY
CORK 420,000

▲ A bridge spans the River Lee in the centre of Cork. The city grew up around the river and on the surrounding hillsides.

Urban and Rural Life

Ireland is not a particularly crowded country. It has, on average, only about 50 people for every square kilometre of territory. As in many other countries, people are tending to live more now in cities and towns than in the country.

Since the 1980s the population of Ireland has been slowly increasing. People who had previously sought work abroad have been returning to their homeland to find new opportunities there. However, Ireland's population of around 3.7 million is still far below what it was in the 1840s, when it stood at around 6.5 million. Then, many people went abroad to escape famine, and others followed them in search of a better future.

Today, as a result, millions of Americans, Britons, Canadians and Australians are of Irish descent. Many of them still take part in Irish customs and traditions.

Millions

▲ Population changes over the last 100 years.

Male Female

Jagged cliffs, rough sea and sheep grazing on open ground are familiar sights in coastal areas of Ireland. ▼

Modern apartments and stone crofts

Whereas most people in Ireland once lived in the countryside, well over half now live in the towns. About a third of the population lives in or around the capital city, Dublin. There, people commute by bus or light railway to get to their places of work in offices or factories. In the evenings they may go out to a pub, restaurant, cinema, theatre or club, before returning home to their house or flat on the outskirts of town.

In the countryside, people live in small villages and work on the land. The traditional croft, or country farmhouse, was made of stone and had a low, thatched roof. Some families still live like this, especially in the west of the country, but many rural houses are now made of brick. Hotels and public houses, or pubs, where families can eat and drink, are the centre of village social life.

Farming and Fishing

Ireland has always been a farming country. Meat, milk and cheeses are still among the country's main exports. Fishing, too, has always formed part of the traditional Irish way of life.

Less than one-sixth of Ireland's farmland is cultivated for growing crops. The rest mainly serves as pasture for grazing animals. In the midlands, cattle are reared mostly for their beef, while dairy cattle are more often found in the south. Sheep provide both meat and wool, and can be seen across the country grazing on mountainsides and hills. Ireland is well-known for its thoroughbred horses. The Curragh plain, in County Kildare, south-west of Dublin, has a horse-racing tradition that goes back more than 2,000 years.

The best cultivated land is in the east and south-east, which receive less rain than the west. Barley, wheat, oats, potatoes, turnips and sugar beet are the major crops. In County Wexford, in the south-east, farmers also grow fruits such as strawberries.

Fishing

Compared to agriculture, the fishing industry is small, but it is expanding. In addition to deep-sea fish, large numbers of lobsters, crayfish, prawns, mussels and oysters are caught near the coasts. Salmon and trout are fished in rivers, lakes and mountain streams. Some fish are bred on fish farms.

Horse mackerel, mackerel and herring top the list of the fishing catch. Most fish are caught at sea, but fish farms have been built in some coastal bays and river mouths. ▶▶

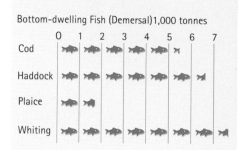

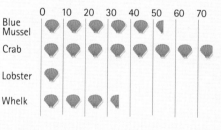

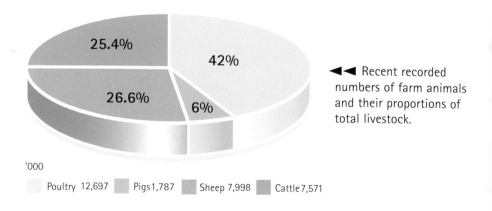

'000

Poultry 12,697   Pigs 1,787   Sheep 7,998   Cattle 7,571

◀◀ Recent recorded numbers of farm animals and their proportions of total livestock.

Farming and Fishing

The most common cereal crop is barley, from which the Irish make whiskey and stout beer. These alcoholic drinks are among Ireland's main exports.

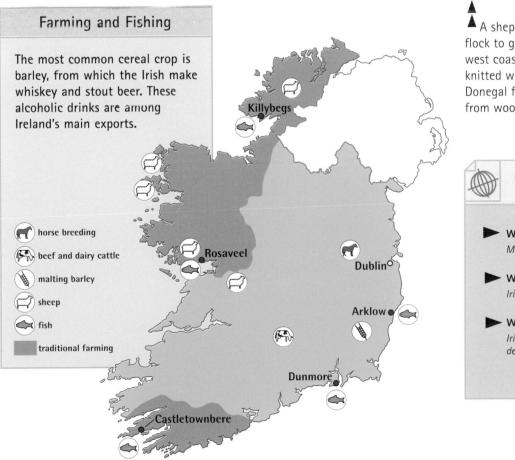

- horse breeding
- beef and dairy cattle
- malting barley
- sheep
- fish
- traditional farming

Killybegs

Rosaveel

Dublin

Arklow

Dunmore

Castletownbere

▲ A shepherd in County Mayo takes his flock to graze. The Aran Islands off the west coast are world-famous for their knitted woollen garments, as is County Donegal for its tweed, a cloth woven from wool.

Web Search ►►

► **www.irlgov.ie/marine**
Marine and natural resources.

► **www.bim.ie**
Irish Sea Fisheries Board.

► **www.cfb.ie**
Irish Central Fisheries Board, which deals with inland fisheries.

Resources and Industry

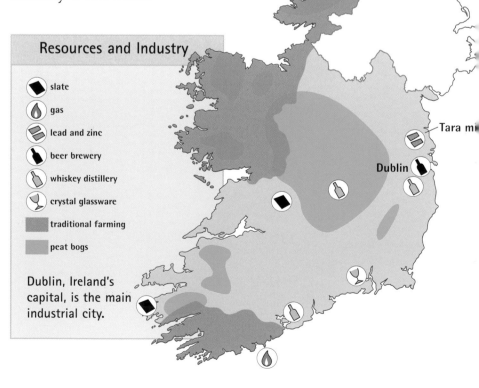

Peat Bogs

Today, peat-burning power stations produce more than one-tenth of Ireland's electricity.

Peat is plant material that has been buried in wet, boggy ground for many thousands of years and has never completely rotted. It is rich in carbon and makes an excellent fuel.

Today in Ireland many more people work in factories than on farms. The growth of tourism in Ireland has also created many jobs in hotels and other service industries. Tourism and the sale of manufactured goods abroad are major contributors to Ireland's successful economy.

Mining also contributes to the country's wealth. Ireland is one of Europe's leading exporters of the mineral zinc. Tara Mine, in County Meath, is the largest lead and zinc mine in Europe. The building material gypsum is also mined in large quantities in Ireland.

Energy

Other minerals, such as natural gas and coal, are sources of energy. Ireland's biggest gas field is at Kinsale Head, off the south coast of County Cork. However, supplies will not last and a new pipeline to bring gas to Ireland from Scotland has already been built.

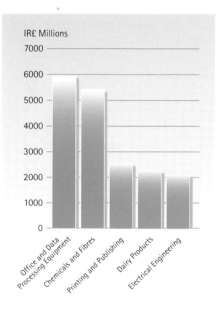

IR£ Millions

7000	
6000	
5000	
4000	
3000	
2000	
1000	
0	

Office and Data Processing Equipment / Chemicals and Fibres / Printing and Publishing / Dairy Products / Electrical Engineering

▲ A comparison of the value of goods made by major industries in Ireland.

Resources and Industry

- slate
- gas
- lead and zinc
- beer brewery
- whiskey distillery
- crystal glassware
- traditional farming
- peat bogs

Dublin, Ireland's capital, is the main industrial city.

Tara mi

Dublin

Coal mining takes place in County Tipperary. But coal, too, is in short supply and most of the country's coal and oil have to be imported.

Some energy is provided by nature without having to dig or drill for it. The rivers Shannon, Erne and Liffey have all been harnessed to provide hydroelectric power. Peat is another natural energy source. For centuries, turfs cut from peat bogs have been burned as fuel in the home.

High-technology industry

In recent years, manufacturing and the nation's wealth generally have grown to the point where Ireland has been called 'The Celtic Tiger'. The manufacture of electronics, particularly computers, has increased considerably and, along with other manufacturing industries, such as furniture, glassware, food and drink, textiles and clothing, helps to provide many jobs.

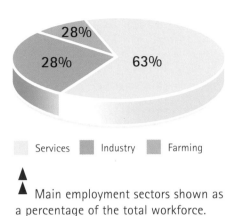

28% 28% 63%

■ Services ■ Industry ■ Farming

▲▲ Main employment sectors shown as a percentage of the total workforce.

In a laboratory, under special lighting conditions, technicians check electronic components. Some of the world's major computer manufacturers have factories in Ireland. ▼▼

Web Search ►►

► www.outokumpu.org
The home page of a company dealing with business, finance and mining, including the Tara zinc mine.

► www.ireland.com/ technology
Information about Ireland's high-technology industries.

► www.esri.ie
Information from Ireland's Economic & Social Research Institute.

Transport

With a relatively small land area and population compared to many of its European neighbours, Ireland's transport needs are served by a mix of private car ownership and public bus and rail networks.

The national airline, Aer Lingus, flies within Ireland and to Europe and the USA. Ferry services across the Irish Sea link Ireland with Britain and the European continent.

As a member of the European Union (EU), Ireland has benefited from grants to improve its transport systems. New bypasses and motorways, partly funded by the EU, have been built to help shorten road journey times and accommodate growing numbers of cars and trucks. In Ireland, vehicles drive on the left side of the road, unlike continental Europe and many other parts of the world.

Ways to Travel

Buses and private cars are the main means of transport in Ireland's bigger towns and cities. Dublin has both buses and the DART (Dublin Area Rapid Transit), a light railway that runs along the coast and into the city between the suburbs of Howth in the north and Bray in the south.

From Rosslare Harbour, near Wexford, ferries provide a link with South Wales and ports in northern France. ▼

Bus and train networks

For passengers using public transport, a national bus service operates across the country, sometimes competing on major routes with private bus companies. Irish Rail runs trains between the main cities and towns. Most of the railway lines radiate out from Dublin. Today, Ireland's rail network totals 1,950 kilometres compared to 92,500 kilometres of roads.

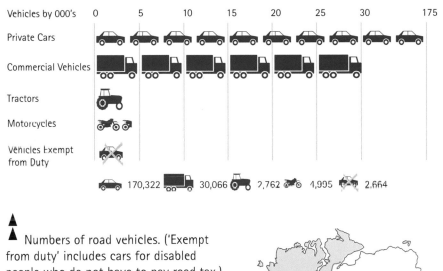

▲ Numbers of road vehicles. ('Exempt from duty' includes cars for disabled people who do not have to pay road tax.)

17

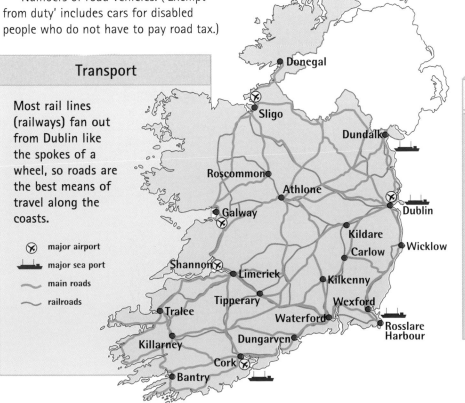

Transport

Most rail lines (railways) fan out from Dublin like the spokes of a wheel, so roads are the best means of travel along the coasts.

- ⊗ major airport
- ⚓ major sea port
- ～ main roads
- ～ railroads

DATABASE

Canal system

Before the 1960s most heavy freight in Ireland was loaded on to barges that travelled across the country on a system of canals. Today, freight is moved mostly by road. Goods being taken to ports such as Dublin, Cork or Waterford to be shipped abroad often travel on huge container lorries.

The two main canals, the Royal and the Grand, which both branch off the River Shannon to the Irish Sea, have been maintained for use by holidaymakers on pleasure barges. In the 1990s the waterway between the rivers Shannon and Erne was also reopened.

Web Search ▶▶

▶ www.aerlingus.ie
The Aer Lingus website.

▶ www.buseireann.ie
Bus timetables and on-line ticket booking from Bus Eirean.

▶ www.irishrail.ie
Irish Rail timetables and travel information.

▶ www.ireland.travel.ie
Tourist travel information.

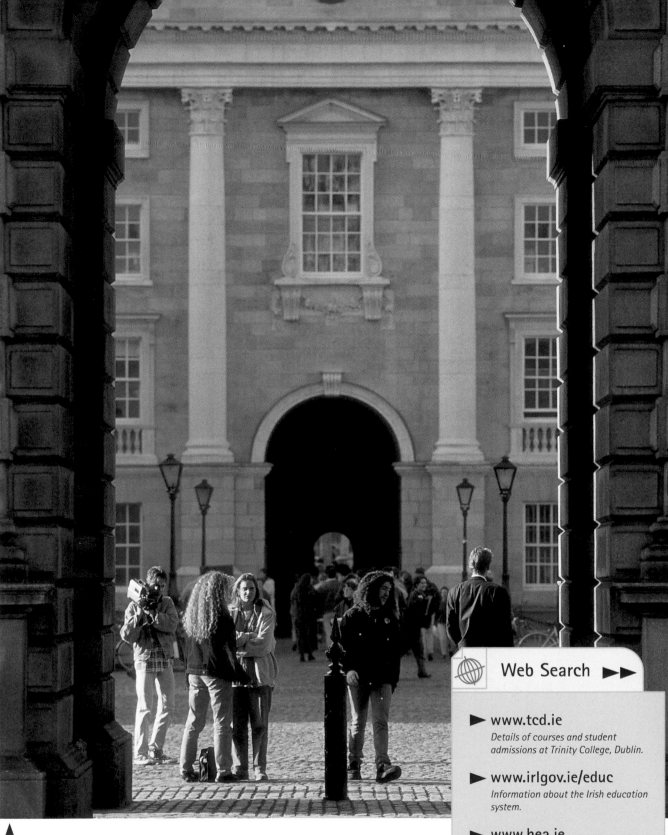

 Students stand and talk in the central square of Trinity College, Dublin. The college was founded in 1592 and is one of the most famous universities in the world.

🌐 Web Search ►►

► **www.tcd.ie**
Details of courses and student admissions at Trinity College, Dublin.

► **www.irlgov.ie/educ**
Information about the Irish education system.

► **www.hea.ie**
Information about higher education in Ireland.

Education

All children in Ireland must attend school between the ages of 6 and 15. Schooling is free. At 15 or 16, children sit their Junior Certificate examination, after which some leave and start work. Others stay on to study for the more advanced Leaving Certificate, and possibly go on afterwards to university.

Boys and girls in their first year at primary, or first-level, school are taught together. After that, they attend separate classes. Even primary school children must do an hour's homework each evening. They must also all learn Irish.

Many children who live in country areas have a long journey to and from school. Special buses collect them from their villages in the morning and return them in the afternoon.

Studying a variety of subjects

Secondary, or second-level, education begins at age 12 or 13. Many secondary schools are run by religious orders such as the Benedictine nuns or Christian Brothers.

Non-religious schools are paid for by the state and local authorities. These schools allow students to take career subjects such as architecture, accountancy and engineering as well as mathematics, English and other academic subjects. Community and comprehensive schools, which are wholly state-funded, also have a curriculum that includes both academic and technical subjects.

Students who finish school at 18, having passed their Leaving Certificate examinations, may go to university or college to follow a degree course or train to be teachers.

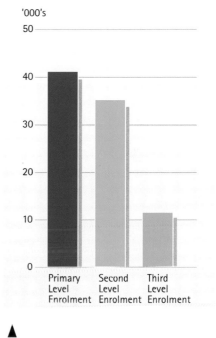

'000's

▲▲ The relative numbers of children and teenagers who attend schools and colleges in Ireland.

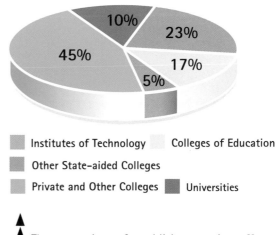

Institutes of Technology   Colleges of Education
Other State-aided Colleges
Private and Other Colleges   Universities

▲ The proportions of establishments that offer students higher, or third level, education.

Sport and Leisure

Many Irish people love sport, whether as participants or spectators. The Irish sports of Gaelic football and hurling have a strong following and are played all over Ireland. The Irish also enjoy horse-riding, golf, boxing, cycling, cricket, fishing, tennis, swimming, sailing and hill-walking.

Hurling is a traditional Irish ball game that is more than 2,000 years old. It is played on a grass pitch between two teams of 15 players, each of whom carries a hurley – a curved stick made of ash wood. The aim is to knock the ball between the upright posts of the opposing team's H-shaped goal. The rules of Gaelic football are similar, but the ball is bigger and players use their hands and feet.

A painting on the side wall of a house shows players during a hurling match and a Gaelic football match, both traditional Irish sports. ▼

Ireland's Racing Tradition

Ireland is world-famous for breeding and training racehorses. There are 25 main racecourses, and race meetings are held throughout the year.

The most famous events are the Irish Derby, run at the Curragh, in County Kildare, in June, and the Irish Grand National, which takes place at Leopardstown, near Dublin, on Easter Monday.

The Irish Derby is a flat-race for three-year-old horses. The National is for mature horses and includes fences.

20

Traditional sports

The home of hurling and Gaelic football is Croke Park in Dublin, a huge stadium where the All-Ireland finals take place every September. Another traditional game is handball, which is similar to squash but players use their hands instead of a racket. Traditional sports are promoted and encouraged by the Gaelic Athletic Association (GAA).

International teams

The Irish Football Association was formed in 1892, and in the following year Ireland played its first international match, against England. Since then, Irish football teams have competed many times in European championships and World Cup competitions, and football has become one of Ireland's most popular sports.

Ireland's football and rugby teams play their home international matches at Lansdowne Road stadium, in Dublin, which holds 50,000 spectators. Ireland also regularly holds international golf tournaments and sends teams of athletes to compete in the Olympic Games.

Web Search ►►

► **www.gaa.ie**
National results for football, hurling, handball and other traditional sports.

► **www.curragh.ie**
Details of horse-racing fixtures.

► **www.fai.ie**
Irish football history, league details and ticket information.

► **www.irlgov.ie/tourism-sport**
Irish government Department of Tourism, Sport and Recreation.

Art students sketch paintings and sculptures in the National Gallery in Dublin. There are more than 80 museums and 40 heritage centres in Ireland. ▼

Daily Life and Religion

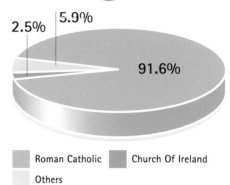

2.5% 5.9%

91.6%

- Roman Catholic
- Church Of Ireland
- Others

Ireland is an increasingly prosperous society with a rising standard of living. Life expectancy is high. The traditional influence of the Roman Catholic Church on daily life is gradually declining.

Although Ireland has no official religion, every city has a cathedral and even a small village is likely to have a church. Mass and other Catholic services are held on Sundays, Saturday evenings and some weekdays. About 3 per cent of the population is Protestant, and there are smaller numbers of Muslims, Jews, Buddhists and Hindus.

▲ Most Irish are Roman Catholics. Protestants belong to the Church of Ireland.

Countryfolk ride through town on traditional horse-drawn carts. Travelling in horse-drawn caravans is a popular way of exploring Ireland. ▼

The working week
Most shops are open from about 9.00 a.m. to 5.00 p.m., Mondays to Saturdays. In Dublin, Cork and several large towns, some shops are open on Sundays, too. Offices and factories are usually closed at weekends. Shopping is a popular weekend pastime. People shop at local markets and large city-centre shopping malls.

Health care
Healthcare in Ireland is free of charge for children and old-age pensioners, and to men and women who are not working or who are on low wages. People in work contribute to the government through a social insurance scheme, which also provides for unemployment pay, pensions for senior citizens and other benefits.

Armed forces
Service in Ireland's army, navy and air corps is voluntary. Army recruits are accepted from the age of 17. The army is the largest of the defence forces, with almost 9,500 serving men and women. Irish troops regularly play an important part in United Nations (UN) operations.

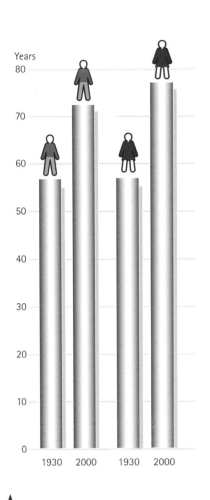

Years

▲
▲ The increase in life expectancy.

▲
▲ Children enter a church in Dublin to take First Communion, when the priest welcomes them into the Roman Catholic community.

🌐 **Web Search** ▶▶

▶ **www.irlgov.ie/defence**
The Irish government's Department of Defence website.

▶ **www.cso.ie**
Ireland's Central Statistical Office has facts and figures on everyday life.

▶ **www.rte.ie**
Irish news plus daily television and radio schedules.

Arts and Media

Irish literature, music and visual arts have been important in European and world culture for many centuries. Today, Irish pop music and dance have added to the artistic expressions for which Ireland is famous.

The Abbey Theatre in Dublin was founded in 1904 by the poet, William Butler Yeats. Classical plays by such Irish playwrights as Richard Brinsley Sheridan, George Bernard Shaw and Oscar Wilde are performed there, as well as more modern Irish dramas, by, for example, Samuel Beckett.

Elsewhere in Dublin a museum honours the memory of another great Irish writer, James Joyce. His most famous novel, *Ulysses*, is set in Dublin and describes events that take place over a single day.

Students play traditional Irish music to shoppers in the centre of Dublin. ▼

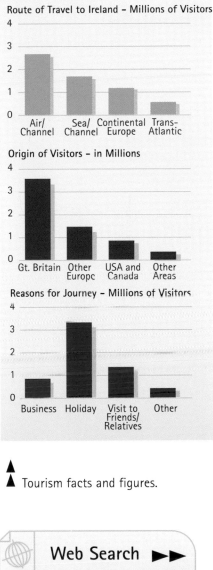

◄◄ Powerscourt in County Wicklow, with its country house and gardens, is a popular tourist attraction.

Route of Travel to Ireland – Millions of Visitors

Origin of Visitors – in Millions

Reasons for Journey – Millions of Visitors

▲ Tourism facts and figures.

Tourism and newspapers

Ireland's many museums and art galleries, historic castles like Blarney, old country houses and scenery consisting of peat bogs, lakes and mountains are attracting more and more tourists. In 2000, over 6 million people visited Ireland.

Ireland has six daily national newspapers, all of which are published in English. The most popular are the *Irish Times* and *Irish Independent*. The *Irish Times*, which sells 112,600 copies every day, includes weekly columns in Irish.

Television and radio

Some television and radio broadcasts are also in Irish. The Irish-language television channel TG4 attracts 335,000 viewers every day, while its fellow radio station, Raidió na Gaeltachta, also has a nationwide audience. Viewers and listeners have a wide choice of programmes, including transmissions by satellite or cable.

Web Search ►►

► www.ireland.com
Irish Times world and Irish news.

► www.independent.ie
Irish Independent and Sunday Independent news and features.

► www.visitdublin.com
Tourist information about Dublin.

Government

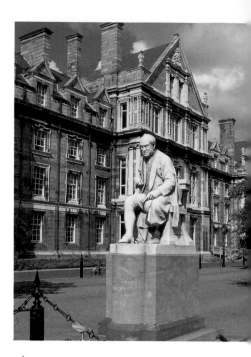

Ireland is an independent democratic republic governed by the Irish parliament. It has a written constitution that guarantees the rights and freedom of all citizens.

The official head of the Irish state is the president, who is elected by the people to serve for seven years. The power to make laws lies not with the president, but with parliament. A member of parliament must be 21 or over, but to vote a person need be only 18.

The leader of the political party that wins the most seats in an election is appointed by the president as Taoiseach (prime minister) of the new government. On the advice of the Taoiseach (pronounced 'Tee-shock'), the president also appoints the other government ministers. The parties represented in parliament include Fine Gail, the Labour Party, Sinn Féin and the Green Party.

▲ Trinity College was founded by the English in 1592. Until recently, it was a symbol of the Irish struggle of independence from Britain.

The Four Courts building, standing on the north bank of the River Liffey in Dublin, houses the government's legal offices. ▼

Local Government

Irish counties have locally elected councils to run services such as health, housing and water supply.

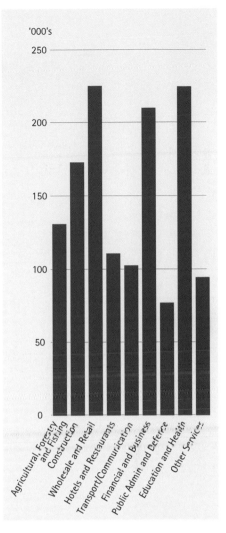

▲▲ Workforces for major government areas of employment and industry.

The government's role

The government's major responsibilities include controlling public spending and raising taxes. Over the past few years, the government has tried to increase spending by 10 per cent to more than £16 billion, with the greatest increases of 40 per cent going to education and 35 per cent to health. Compared to other European countries, Ireland spends very little on defence, only 1.05 per cent of its national wealth.

DATABASE

Irish Parliament

The nation's parliament consists of a 'lower house' called the Dáil (pronounced 'Doil') and an 'upper house'.

The Dáil's 166 members, most of whom represent political parties, are elected to serve for five years.

Parliament's upper house, the Senead (pronounced 'Sha-nad'), has 60 members, 11 of whom are chosen by the Taoiseach, and others who are elected by various public bodies.

Web Search ▶▶

▶ www.irl.gov/info.htm
Irish government information links.

▶ www.irl.gov.ie/Alphaindex.htm
An alphabetic index to Irish government information sources.

▶ www.askireland.com
General information about Ireland.

Place in the World

Chronology of Historical Events

1607 Ulster plantation. Start of British policy of settling Scots and English in the north of Ireland and confiscating Irish people's land.

1845–9 Famine brought about by the failure of the potato crop. Some 800,000 people died of starvation or disease. Over a million emigrated to England, Canada and the USA.

1916 Easter Rising. Armed rebellion in Dublin against British rule is brutally suppressed.

1919 Birth of the Irish Republican Army (IRA), a paramilitary group pledged to fight British rule. A Declaration of Independence was drafted and read out in Irish, English and French at a meeting of the first Irish Assembly.

1920 Government of Ireland Act divides the island into the Irish Free State, with dominion status, and Northern Ireland.

1922–3 Civil war in which the Free State army defeats republicans opposed to partition.

1949 Ireland becomes a republic.

1955 Ireland joins the United Nations.

1973 Ireland joins the European Community.

1985 Anglo–Irish Agreement signed by Taoiseach Garret FitzGerald and UK prime minister Margaret Thatcher.

1998 Good Friday Agreement peace plan for Northern Ireland approved by referendum.

1999 Ireland joins the European Monetary Union.

Ireland has gained a significant place in the world, not least because there are so many people of Irish descent living in many different countries.

Ireland plays a big part in helping United Nations (UN) peacekeeping forces in troubled nations and has been a member of the European Union (EU) since 1973. In 1999, Ireland joined the European Monetary Union and from 2002 the euro is the new national unit of currency.

In 1990, the value of Irish goods sold abroad was 15 per cent higher than that of imported goods, but by 2000 that figure had risen to 55 per cent. Ireland's biggest trading surplus is with Germany, France and other EU countries of mainland Europe. Between them, these countries buy nearly three times as much from Ireland as Ireland buys from them.

Irish independence

Ireland gained partial independence from the UK in 1921, after a violent struggle, and later, in 1949, became a fully-fledged republic. However, 6 of the 32 Irish counties remained a province of the UK called Northern Ireland. The partition led in 1922 to civil war in the newly independent state. It also led to lasting bitterness and unrest in the North.

City Hall in Belfast, the capital of Northern Ireland. ▶▶

◄◄ Celtic crosses and tower at Clonmacnoise Abbey in County Offaly. The ruins date from the 10th century.

IR£ 52.23 Million

EXPORTS

IMPORTS

IR£ 34.41 Million

IR£millions

22

12

10

8

6

4

2

0

Great Britain and N.Ireland

Other EU Countries

USA

Rest of World

■ Imports ■ Exports

Web Search ►►

► **www.ireland.org/irl_hist/default.htm**
Information about Irish history from ancient times to the present day.

► **www.irlgov.ie/iveagh**
The Irish government's Department of Foreign Affairs, with links to and details of Ireland's European Union policies.

Peace and cooperation

In 1985, the Republic of Ireland was officially consulted for the first time by Britain over the future of Northern Ireland. In the 1990s, the Republic assisted in setting up a peace plan for the North that replaced direct rule from Britain with an all-party elected assembly. The plan also provided for greater cross-border cooperation between the Republic and the North.

In May 1998 the peace plan was voted on and approved by populations on both sides of the border.

▲ Annual trading figures and trading partners around the world.

Area:
70,282sq km

Population size:
3.7 million

Capital city:
Dublin (population 1,058,264)

Other major cities:
Cork (127,187), Galway (57,241), Limerick (52,039), Waterford (42, 540)

Longest river:
River Shannon (260km)

Highest mountain:
Carrantuohill (1,041m)

Currency:
From 2002 euros; before that punts (IR£)

Flag:
The flag was introduced in 1848. The design was based on the French tricolour. The green band represents the Gaelic and Anglo-Norman elements of the people. The orange stands for the Protestants, who supported William of Orange. The white band between the green and the orange signifies a lasting truce between the 'Orange' and the 'Green'.

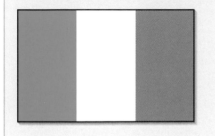

Languages:
Official languages: Irish, English

Natural resources:
zinc, lead, gypsum, natural gas, peat, silver

Major exports:
chemicals, machinery and computer equipment, meat, dairy products, manufactured goods, drinks and tobacco, raw materials, minerals

Some national holidays and festivals:
17 March
St Patrick's Day, a national holiday. Most people wear a shamrock and take part in street parades.
16 June
Bloomsday, Dublin. Readings and re-enactments of scenes from James Joyce's *Ulysses*.
early July
Strawberry Fair, Enniscorthy, County Wexford. Strawberries, Irish dancing, horse- and greyhound racing.

10–12 August
Puck Fair, Killorgin, County Kerry. Merriment surrounding a goat coronation ceremony.
late August
'Rose of Tralee' Festival, Tralee, County Kerry. Competition among girls for the title of the 'Rose'.
mid-September
Galway Oyster Festival. Street theatre and oyster-opening contests.
First two weeks in October
Theatre Festival, Dublin. Performances of plays from Ireland and around the world.
25–26 December
Christmas Day and St Stephen's (Boxing) Day.

Official religion:
none

Other religions: Roman Catholic 91.6%, Protestant 2.5%, Muslim, Jewish and others 5.9%

Glossary

BALANCE OF TRADE
The difference between the value of exported and imported goods.

BOG
An area of ground that is wet all year round. *See* peat.

CELTS
People who came to Ireland from Europe and dominated much of Europe during the 1st millennium BC.

COALITION
An alliance.

DÁIL
The elected house of the Irish parliament. *See also* Senead.

DOMINION
Self-governing territory of the former British Empire, such as the Irish Free State before it became a republic.

ECONOMY
The basis on which a country's wealth is organized.

GAELTACHT
Regions of Ireland where Irish is the first spoken language and Gaelic traditions are still strong.

GROSS DOMESTIC PRODUCT (GDP)
The value of all the goods and services produced by a country over a year or other period.

HURLING
Traditional Irish field game played between two teams of 15 players who use a curved stick, or hurley, to strike a ball and score goals.

HYDROELECTRIC POWER (HEP)
Electricity generated from the energy of water movement.

INDEPENDENCE
Governing of a country by its own people.

IRISH REPUBLICAN ARMY (IRA)
A paramilitary group created in 1919 to fight for Ireland's independence from British rule.

PEAT
Dark-brown, solid material that forms in bogs as a result of the build-up and compression of dead, rotting plants. Also called turf.

REPUBLIC
An independent country whose head of state is an elected president.

SENEAD
The unelected, upper house of the Irish parliament.

SHAMROCK
A three-leafed clover, the emblem of Ireland.

ST PATRICK
The patron saint of Ireland who spread Christianity across the country in the 5th century AD.

SUBSISTENCE FARMING
Growing enough food to feed the farmer's household but no more. It is common in the Gaeltacht region of Ireland.

WHISKEY
Traditional Irish spirit made from barley and distilled three times.

Index

armed forces 22

barley 12, 13, 31
bog 6, 15, 25, 31
buses 16, 17, 19

canals 17
Carrantuohill 6, 30
cars and roads 16, 17
cattle 12
Celts 4, 8, 31
climate 4, 7
coal 14, 15
coastline 4, 6
constitution 9, 26
Cork, County 6, 8, 14, 24
crops 12, 13
currency 28, 30

Donegal, County 4, 6, 13
Dublin 11, 14, 16, 17, 18, 19, 20, 21, 23, 24, 26, 30

economy 14, 28, 29
education and schools 9, 19, 22, 27
elections 26, 27
electricity 14, 15
employment 14, 15, 27
energy 14, 15
European Union (EU) 16, 28
exports 12, 13, 14, 29, 30

famine 11, 28
farming 4, 12, 13
ferry services 16

festivals 30
fishing 8, 12, 13
flag 30
foreign trade 28, 31

Gaeltacht 9, 31

healthcare 22, 27
horse-racing 12, 20
hurling 20, 21, 31
hydroelectric power (HEP) 15, 31

imports 15, 28, 29
independence 4, 9, 28, 31
Irish Republican Army (IRA) 28, 31
Irish Sea 4, 17

Joyce, James 4, 24

landscape 4, 6, 11
land use 4, 12
language 4, 8–9, 30
life expectancy 22, 23
Liffey, River 7, 15,
Limerick 7, 30
livestock numbers 12
local government 27

manufacturing 14, 15
mining 14, 15
museums and galleries 21, 25
music 4, 24

natural resources 14–15, 30
newspapers 25

Northern Ireland 4, 20, 28, 29

Olympic Games 21

parliament 26, 27, 31
peat 6, 14, 15, 31
political parties 26
population 8, 9, 11, 30

radio and television 25
railways 16, 17
rainfall 6, 7, 12
religion 19, 22–3, 30
republic 4, 26, 28, 29, 31

Shannon, River 7, 15, 17, 30
sheep 11, 12, 13
shops and offices 22
sport 20–1
standard of living 22

taxes 27
tourism 14, 25
town and country 11
traditional homes 4, 11
Trinity College 18, 26

United Kingdom (UK) 4, 9, 28
United Nations (UN) 22, 28

whiskey 13, 14, 31
wildlife 6
wool 12, 13

Yeats, William Butler 4, 24